Baby Shower Ideas

Your Fun and Simple Guide to Baby Shower Planning

Denee Lewis

D1264560

Liability Disclaimer

By reading this book, you assume all risks associated with using the advice given below, with a full understanding that you, solely, are responsible for anything that may occur as a result of putting this information into action in any way, and regardless of your interpretation of the advice.

You further agree that our company cannot be held responsible in any way for the success or failure of your shower as a result of the information presented in this book.

Terms of Use

You are given a non-transferable, "personal use" license to this book. You cannot distribute it or share it with other individuals.

Also, there are no resale rights or private label rights granted when purchasing this book. In other words, it's for your own personal use only.

Baby Shower Ideas

Your Fun and Simple Guide to Baby Shower Planning

Table of Contents

The Shower Process Begins

If you are holding this book in your hand then chances are you are now responsible for planning and throwing a baby shower! Take a deep breath and know that everything is going to be ok. Whether you are a family member or close friend, planning and throwing a baby shower is indeed a huge responsibility, but it is a huge honor as well. Don't let all the details overwhelm you. You have a wonderful resource in your hand that will give ideas, tips, decorating suggestions, recipes, and much more. You can not only throw a baby shower, you can throw an **amazing** baby shower and manage to have fun in the process!!

The birth of a child is always an occasion for joy. The new mother you are holding this shower for is feeling a lot of joy right now, plus countless other emotions as well. That joy should always be at the forefront of everything that is done for the shower. Envision the day she sits at your shower and opens each gift, and know that you helped create a wonderful atmosphere of fun, excitement, and most importantly love and joy.

If you have never tried to plan and organize a baby shower before...don't worry, you CAN do it. If you have had issues throwing a shower in the past, know that this shower is a fresh start and you will do just fine. Now keep in mind though, once you throw a fabulous baby shower, you may just be in demand to do more!!!

As you make your way through this book, bear in mind that the suggestions in here are just that...suggestions. Take them and use them the way that is best for you. Use the tips in here as a guide for creating a special day for the mother-to-be, and all her friends and family that attend the shower. Some of the ideas in here you'll want to use exactly and others won't fit with what you need to do. Don't worry if you apply only some of what you read here. A helpful suggestion that I would recommend is read the book completely through at least once before you start implementing things from it. You may find things covered in the later sections of the book that would be helpful to you as you start your planning stage.

Use your common sense, and remember: baby showers aren't supposed to be regarded like a trip to the dentist; they are supposed to be enjoyable. You enjoy the process too. The more you enjoy it, the more that feeling is going to be communicated to your mom-to-be and guests.

This book is divided into four sections. The first part is the planning stage of the shower, the second part is the actual details of the shower itself, the third part is some frequently asked questions and other general tips regarding showers, and the fourth part is some helpful checklists that you can use as you plan. Ideally, the planning stage should begin months, or in the very least, several weeks before the shower is to be held. In the planning stage you will answer six major questions

- Who should plan/host the shower?
- When should the shower be?
- Whom should I invite?
- Should a gift registry be used?
- Where will the shower be held?
- What is my budget going to be?

Once these questions are answered then you will move on to the actual details of the shower. These will be covered in the second part of the book. Topics covered are:

- Themes/Decorations
- Setting Up Your Room
- Games
- Food
- Opening Gifts
- Clean Up

The third section of the book deals with frequently asked questions regarding baby showers such as hosting couples showers or adoption showers.

The fourth section is some checklists you can choose to use in your shower planning. Hopefully they will give you some useful guides to follow to help keep yourself organized. If you are reading this book as a digital e-book you can go online and access the checklists at http://babyshowerplanning.org/planner/planners.pdf

So let's get started planning this baby shower!

Part 1: Planning the Shower

The planning stage of the baby shower is the absolute most critical part of the process. If you have ever attended a baby shower, the whole process honestly may look very simple. Show up, socialize, play some games, eat some food, watch mom open the gifts, and go home.

Behind all of those simple things however, are many, many details that have to be thought of. What is the best day for everybody to show up? What time of day? Where should the shower be held? How many guests will be coming? What games should be played? The details go on and on and for your shower to be successful you need to ask all of those questions and make sure you have the answers.

To an outside observer all baby showers may look very similar, but in truth all are unique. Any time that you are dealing with people and their personalities then you have a unique situation.

When planning a baby shower you generally start with the broad categories first. Who, when and where are three key questions that must be answered before anything else can be determined. Once you get those factors determined then you can start narrowing in on all the fine details that will make your shower a success.

You cannot over plan. A baby shower is a great event that creates a lot of joy. There are quite a few details to put together however and it does require some time if you want to host the best shower possible. The best thing you can do for yourself is give yourself as much time as you can. Throwing a shower together at the last minute can absolutely be done, but not only is much more stress is going to be involved in the process, you also run the risk of missing or overlooking some of those all important details. So give yourself as much time as you possibly can and plan, plan, plan.

Also, especially if you are planning a very large or elaborate shower then try and recruit some quality helpers. Designating tasks to people that you trust will take a lot of pressure off you.

So let's get into the planning section and start answering those all important questions.

Who Should Throw the Shower?

Formal etiquette for baby showers used to say that relatives should avoid throwing the baby shower because it would give the appearance that the family was asking for presents.

Thankfully, in our current times, etiquette and formality have eased and the question of who should throw the shower can be fairly simply answered as: Anybody who is capable to do so that is not the expectant parents. Don't worry about etiquette and tradition and do worry about the most important thing: Creating a positive environment for the mother-to-be to share her happiness with the people that she is close to. Whoever you are that is holding this book, whether, aunt, cousin, sister, mother, friend or co-worker, just focus on giving the mom-to-be a great shower and know that you will do great!

The Time Factor: When Should the Shower Happen?

This is a very important question to ask in the planning state of a baby shower and one of the key questions that must be answered before determining anything else. Traditionally, a baby shower is usually held a couple of months before the baby is born. Sometimes showers are held closer to the due date, but it gets a little riskier to do so. Babies often have their own timetable about when they want to arrive and if you have a shower too close to the due date then the baby may decide he wants to throw a kink in your plans!

Now just because something is tradition, however, does not always mean that it is set in stone. There are always factors and variables that can occur in any situation and those must come into play when determining the date of the shower. Every shower is unique, so let's just look at some of the most common and important variables that you should consider in your planning. Once you know these, you'll easily be able to determine when the baby shower should be held.

The Parents and Other Important Guests

Let's start with the expectant parents. The most important factor of determining when to hold the shower is finding out when it is convenient for the mother-to-be...or both parents if holding a couples shower...to be able to attend. They should be the guiding force behind the main decision and should be consulted. A second import factor is whether there are going to be family members at the shower. If you are throwing a work baby shower then you don't need to worry too much about this factor. If however you are holding a shower and are planning on inviting family members, then make sure that key family members can be there. A beloved grandmother or aunt may be someone that the mother-to-be would desperately want to have at her shower and it would be important to make sure that it is held when those special family members can be there.

The Season

December is one of the absolute busiest months of the year. During that time people are usually shopping, cooking, and often trying to plan their own Christmas get-togethers with family. If at all possible this month is not the best month to hold a baby shower. You run into the definite possibility that not as many people will be able to attend if you hold the shower in December. People probably wouldn't be able to relax and have as good a time either. If they are trying to squeeze in multiple commitments during this month, another get-together could be very stressful. So if the shower would naturally fall during this particular month you might want to go with an earlier shower.

Weather conditions in the winter are another factor you might have to consider when planning on the date of a shower. If you live in an area that gets a lot of snow and ice in the winter time then you definitely want to think about that when considering your shower date. Yes, life does go on in the winter and people have to get out to work and other places in bad weather conditions, but if not absolutely necessary to do so, then the shower should probably be held at a time that would be more pleasant for everyone to get out.

Boy or Girl Gifts

Ultrasounds have completely changed the course of baby showers. Many years ago, it wasn't possible to know whether the baby was a boy or a girl until the moment that he or she was born. Now ultrasounds are possible and it is easy to know months before the baby is born whether it will be a boy or a girl. While some parents still want a surprise, many choose to go ahead and find out so they can decorate their nursery in a specific way or go ahead and buy frilly dresses or adorable little suits. If you know that the expectant parents to be are indeed going to have an ultrasound done, you might want to wait until after this to hold the shower. That way you can let the attendees know if the baby is going to be a boy or girl and that gives them the option on whether they want to buy gender specific gifts. Always keep in mind however that ultrasounds have been wrong before and so there is always the possibility of a surprise!

Post-Birth Baby Showers

If finding the perfect time to hold the shower before the baby is born seems to be a daunting task, don't be afraid to consider asking the parents if they would like to have the shower after the baby is born. Post-birth baby showers are becoming quite popular indeed because then of course it gives everybody the opportunity admire the guest of honor! Mom gets a perfect opportunity to relax and enjoy herself for a few minutes because she will of course find herself surrounded by eager, clamoring volunteers to help take care of the baby! Waiting until after the baby is born is also a sure fire way for people to be able to buy gender specific gifts without any risk of there being a mistake.

Sending Out Invitations

Okay, here's the part that can get awkward and complicated. This is often the part of planning a baby shower that makes people dread accepting the responsibility in the first place. It's one of the most important questions that has to be asked and the one people worry the most about. *"Whom do I invite?"*

Knowing who to invite to a shower can in some cases be complicated. Unfortunately, family situations may not always be simple due to divorces, re-marriages, and feelings. Knowing how to navigate these murky areas can often feel like diving into shark infested waters without a protective cage. To keep yourself sane, the key factor in deciding the guest list is to go to the one you are holding the shower for. Work with the mother (and ideally, the father) to-be in order to decide who should attend, and who should be left off the list. This is a delicate scenario and can cause a number of minor headaches (even some major ones).

Sometimes it may just not be possible to invite every single person that may want to attend. If a shower gets too large it can easily get out of hand both financially and in terms of planning. Sometimes decisions have to be made as to who to invite and who not to invite and working with the parents in this matter will ease a great deal of your stress.

Find out from the mother-to-be if she is going to be having multiple showers. If she has other friends that are going to be giving her showers as well then that may be a help in determining who to invite on your guest list. Certain key family members such as the grandmothers or aunts may indeed come to all showers but if friends are going to be attending other baby showers then that could be a balancing factor for your guest list. Always get the final approval of the mother-to-be regarding the guest list before you move on to sending out invitations.

Once the guest list has finally been determined, then it will be time to send out the invitations. One crucial suggestion in the invitation process is to get them sent out as early as you possibly can. Giving people plenty of advance notice of the shower date will ensure that as many people come as possible. Eight weeks in advance would be good for sending out invitations and if the guest list is going to be really large you might even want to consider ten weeks.

First, you want to make sure to give the ones invited enough time that they can change their plans if they need or want to. If you don't provide them with enough notice, even if they *want* to change their existing plans, they might not be able to.

Second, you want to give people time to RSVP...confirm their attendance...back to you. Getting as many confirmations back as possible will give you an accurate idea of how many are coming and will make planning food and games all that much easier.

Now, let's discuss the best type of invitation that is the most efficient to send out. When you send out an invitation that includes an RSVP, you are asking someone to respond back to you. You can always hope that person will do so and it is indeed very polite for her to do so. However, just because someone does not RSVP does not always mean that she isn't coming to the shower. An RSVP is a request but many people don't always respond to that request. Someone who has a hectic schedule may wait until the very last minute to decide if she is going to go to the shower or not, and knowing that she is going to wait until the last minute she may ignore the RSVP. Sadly, people that aren't invested in all the planning and details that go into creating a great shower don't always realize how much stress they can cause by not sending back an RSVP.

Now, is there a perfect solution to this issue? Unfortunately, no, there is not. However, in the invitation you send out, you can go a long way in making it crystal clear that you would like a response back from someone whether she is planning on attending or not. One of the easiest ways to do this is to include a self-addressed stamped envelope within each invitation. Giving people an absolute and very convenient means to respond back can ensure more people do so.

The wording of the invitation itself is also an important factor. Make it clear that you would like people to respond whether they are coming or not. Listed on the next page is a sample of what you might want to send out:

Dear Jane,

You are warmly invited to attend a baby shower for our friend Ann!

The shower will be held on April 17th at 2:30pm. It will be held at my home, which is at 321 Jones Street. It's just one block east of Smith Avenue, and ample parking is available on the street. If you need directions, please call me at 555-1234.

We'd like to have a sense of how many of Ann's friends will be able to attend. Could you please fill out this form below by checking the appropriate box, and then mail it to me in the self-addressed stamped envelope provided? Please send it to me by March 27th. Thank you so much!

(Please check one)

I will be attending Ann's baby shower on April 17th at 2:30pm.

I regretfully will not be able to attend the baby shower.

*** Remember: Please mail before March 27th in the self-addressed stamped envelope provided. THANK YOU! ***

You can change the template to any variation you want to. This is just a simple little sample that highlights the things that you should ask: whether an invitee is attending, or whether an invitee *isn't*. It is very simple and straightforward and there isn't a grey area. You are asking someone to definitively tell you yes or no whether she is coming or not.

Invitation Ideas

Now that you know some good ideas for the wording of your invitation, let's talk a little about the style of invitation.

Stock Invitations – You can go to any party planning store or general department store and find invitations for your shower. All you would have to do would be to fill them out. If you go with stock invitations you would be restricted to the layout of the invitation that you buy, but with as many varieties as there are you shouldn't have too much difficulty being able to find something that you need.

Homemade Invitations – If you are a creative type of person you might want to make your own invitations to the shower. Invitations can be straightforward cards that you design and print out on your computer, or you can get creative and cut them into decorative shapes. If you are planning a theme for your shower you can design your invitations to go with your theme. Invitations are only limited by your imagination. Listed below are a few suggestions of different types of invitations that you might be able to do:

- **Diaper Invitations** – Either decorate your rectangle invitations with pictures or stickers of diapers or cut your invitations out in the shape of a diaper
- **Raindrop Invitations** – Cut each invitation out in the shape of a raindrop
- **Blue/Pink Invitations** – If you know if the baby is a boy or girl you can send out blue or pink invitations. These invitations would be perfect if you were doing a Boy/Girl theme for your shower
- **Baby Feet Invitations** – Cut each invitation out in the shape of a baby's foot.

The RSVP

Now, if you have a small guest list that is easily manageable, you may want to skip doing an RSVP by mail and simply call each person and ask if she will be attending. This is a very personal approach and it not only gives you a clear understanding of who is and is not attending; it also gives the ones you are inviting a chance to ask any questions they might have for you. This will give you the opportunity to share any information you might have such as whether or not the baby is a boy or a girl and whether or not the mother is registered anywhere.

A phone campaign is very personal, but if the guest list is large then this may not be practical. If you have some dependable people able to help you with phone calls then it might still be possible to do a phone campaign even with a large guest list. If not, then mailing would be the way to go. Even with a very clear invitation you still might have an unexpected person or two show up. However, the more detail you can include in your planning communication then the higher the chance that people will respond back to you. In your invitation just be sure to include any information that you feel might be pertinent for people to know regarding the shower. If you want to point people towards a gift registry then you might want to include that on the invitation. Let's talk about gift registries next.

Gift Registries

Gift registries can relieve a lot of stress from people's lives when it comes to buying a baby gift. Everybody that buys a baby gift wants to buy something that will be special and also useful. Walking into a baby super store is often like walking into another land. Surrounded by clothes, diapers, creams, blankets, bibs, and various other things; it can be an overwhelming decision in knowing exactly what is the right thing to buy? Even as you buy something you are plagued by the thought that ten other people might be buying the very thing you are. That is where gift registries can be so useful. They answer very definitively the questions:

- **What will the parents-to-be want as a gift?**

- **What gift items have already been purchased by other invitees?**

- **What price range is appropriate?**

So with all of this evidence in favor of gift registries, why might someone choose not use one? Well, there are a couple of reasons.

The simplest reason is one of *preference*. Some parents may not want to put down a list of things and make people feel like they are *expected* to buy them. They know that people might see that perfect little outfit and absolutely want to buy it, but may feel like they can't if they feel like they should get items from a registry instead. Some people like to do handmade gifts and they may want to sew the baby something or even carve a crib or bassinet from wood. Parents may want to give no hint of expectations when it comes to receiving gifts and thereby wish to avoid using a registry.

Another reason is one of cost. Baby items, especially some of the larger ones that parents do indeed need the most, can be very expensive. It could be awkward for the parents to register for items that they feel could be outside of people's price range. If the registry isn't large or they only register at one store then it is possible that smaller, cheaper priced things could be bought quickly and then people that are buying gifts later could be left with gifts that more expensive then they wanted to pay.

The decision on whether or not to use a gift registry will be ultimately up to the parents and you should honor any decision they make. Gift registries do make gift buying easier and if parents-to-be are worried about the cost issue, you as the shower planner can go a long way in easing their mind over the situation. You through your invitations can gently nudge people towards the idea of going in together to purchase some of those larger, more expensive items. This will help people from going over budget and it will ensure that the parents get the gifts that they truly do want and need.

If the parents do want a gift registry to be used then make sure that is communicated to everyone who is invited to the shower. You can include the details on the invitation or you might want to send an e-mail or call people on the phone. Be sure to make yourself available to people to be able to ask questions regarding the gift registry. Effective communication with people is always the way to ensure that things go smoothly.

Where to Hold the Shower

This is the last main question that must be determined when planning a baby shower. The biggest factor in determining where the shower should be held will be the size of the guest list. The most common location for a shower is, of course, a home. Generally, the person that is planning the shower is also hosting the shower and it is usually their home the shower is held in. If the guest list is very large, however, then one has to ask the question if a home will be large enough to comfortably hold everyone. If the answer is no then shower would need to be held at another location. Banquet halls, fellowship halls at churches, conference rooms, or restaurants are all other places that it would be possible to hold the shower at. Holding the shower at a restaurant can cause an awkward situation so let's talk about that specifically for a moment.

Restaurants

Many restaurants have large rooms that can be reserved for parties and showers so as a size factor they are a comfortable space to hold a shower in. You don't have to worry about food when holding the shower at a restaurant, however that immediately brings up the important and awkward question: Who is responsible for paying for the bill? The answer to that question is the person hosting the shower is responsible for the bill. Asking people to come to a restaurant for a shower and then asking them to pay for their meal is not proper. The only time this might be considered is if an entire group was planning the shower and everybody knew up front that they would be purchasing their own meal. Other than that scenario, it is the responsibility of the person hosting to pay for the costs. Nobody is asked to chip in for the food purchased for a shower in a home and a restaurant would be no different.

As you can imagine holding a shower at a restaurant would be an extremely large expense for one person to manage unless the group was very small. If you have other people that are willing to come along beside you and split the cost then you could consider a restaurant but other than that, you probably want to consider another location. If you do go with a restaurant for the shower be sure and get all the policies and guidelines that the restaurant has in place regarding the use of their location. If you are planning on bringing your own cake make sure you discuss this with the restaurant first. Most places don't have a problem with bringing a special dessert in for certain occasions but always check with them first.

If you hold the shower in any other location besides someone's home then you are going to have to pay to reserve the place. Be sure to factor that into the budget when you are planning the shower. Also, if you are holding the shower in an outside location then you definitely need to make sure that a date and time is locked well in advance. Rearranging the schedule at someone's home would be complicated and stressful; rearranging at an outside location could be downright impossible.

Budget

The budget for your shower is going to flow very naturally from making the decisions on all the key factors that we have discussed so far. Food is most likely going to be your biggest expense so it is crucial that you get your guest list planned out so you will have an estimate in knowing how much you will have to buy. The more elaborate your menu gets, the more costly things will get. As we discussed above, holding the baby shower at any other location besides a home is going to involve payment as well. Decoration cost is going to depend on if you decide to do a theme and how elaborate you want to get. If you are planning on playing games at the shower (these will be discussed in detail further in the book) then you will need to purchase small prizes for the winners of the games.

It is very important that you set your budget early and then stick with it. When you start planning food and shopping for decorations it is so very easy to get caught up in a whirlwind. Baby shower stuff is cute and it is fun and stores that sell it know how to market things very well. If you don't set your budget in stone right from the very beginning you could easily buy things that are not necessary and end up spending twice or three times the amount that you planned. If the shower is going to be large and you are dreaming of elaborate plans, consider asking two or three other people to come along beside you and help split the costs. If this is not possible then remember simple can still be elegant and wonderful. If money is no object, then knock yourself out and have fun!! ☺

Now that you have when, who, where, and most importantly your budget figured out, it is now time to move on to the details of holding the shower. The planning stage is often the most complicated part of the shower because there are numerous factors involved in deciding when to hold the shower and who to invite. The bottom line to remember is you are not going to be able to please every single person in every single situation. The main people you should be focused on are the mother and father to be. People must understand that they are the ones having the baby and the shower is for **them**.

Now, on to the details!!!

Part 2: Details of the Shower

Okay. You've figured out when to hold the shower, where to hold the shower, who to invite, whether or not to use a gift registry, and what your budget is going to be. So that's all there is to it, right? *Hardly!*

Now is the time to think about and manage all the details that will be occurring at the shower. A shower does have a natural flow to it and there are two central things that everything else will naturally revolve around...eating and gift opening. There are still many details that must be worked out however to make sure that everything flows smoothly.

You have already done a great deal of work and you should definitely take a moment and pat yourself on the back. The most complicated factors are behind you and now it is time for those final decisions to help make your shower truly wonderful.

Themes/Decorations

When someone walks into the room on the day of the shower, the decorations will be one of the first things that they see. It will immediately set the tone of the day. Decorating for a shower does not in any way have to be hard. The two words to keep in mind for decorations are festive and fun.

One popular method for decorating at a shower is holding a themed baby shower. This involves setting a certain theme or topic for the shower and then having all the decorations, color schemes, and even in some cases food go along with the theme. This is a fun way to get creative with the shower and it sometimes makes decorating easier since you know exactly what the shower is going to be about. Themes can be as simple as going with all pink for girls or blue for boys or getting as involved as having everybody show up in costumes for the shower.

You can go as simple or as complicated as you like. Anything that is feasible within your budget is fine.
To create a theme, simply have the following items reflect what you've chosen:

☑ **The invitations should themselves reflect the chosen theme (e.g. Teddy Bears)**

☑ **The room should be decorated with items reflecting the theme (e.g. colors, posters, props such as stuffed animals or balloons)**

☑ **The refreshments and food can reflect the theme if desired**

Now, in case you need some help with ideas for a theme listed below are a few examples: (Note – some of these themes involve the guests bringing something to get in on the fun of the theme. Always let them know that participation is voluntary and if they can't afford to do so then to not feel any pressure to participate)

It's A Boy/Girl Theme

This theme is the easiest of all to do and can be done if you already know if the baby is going to be a boy or girl. In this case simply decorate with pink for a girl and blue for a boy. Pink or blue streamers and balloons can be set about the room. The tablecloth, napkins, and plates can all be the theme color and of course, the cake would naturally be decorated with pink or blue. The guests can absolutely get in on the fun by dressing in pink or blue clothes. This theme is a classic but it is fun and there is no stress involved in the planning of it at all.

Stuffed Animal Theme

This is another very simple theme to do. Simply decorate the room with stuffed animals. Teddy bears, puppies, kittens, and any other stuffed animal would all be welcome additions. The colors could be whatever you wanted them to be. Napkins with teddy bears or bunnies would be very easy to find and a cake could be easily be decorated as well. Ask the guests to bring a small stuffed animal with them. When they arrive they can add to the decorations with their animal and then at the end of the day they can all give the stuffed animals to the mother-to-be for the baby!

Diaper Theme

This theme is not only fun it is practical too and will probably make mom and dad very grateful! Color schemes for streamers or balloons can be whatever you want. The cake should be easy to have decorated with a picture of a diaper or safety pin on it. Ask each guest to bring a pack of diapers with them. Encourage them to buy different sized diapers and not just newborn. As the guests arrive the diaper packs can be set about the room as part of the decorations. At the end of the shower they of course will be given to the parents for the baby. I guarantee you they will love this theme and gesture.

Theme: Literary Baby

Books can hold such a special meaning for us as we are growing up. Snuggling in our mom's or dad's arms, as she or he read a story, is for many a cherished childhood memory. As we got older, we discovered the joy of books ourselves. The first time the words "see Spot run" actually clicked in our brains, a door was opened for us into a whole new world. Books allowed us to meet that very silly cat wearing a hat and to question whether green eggs and ham might not be quite delicious after all. As we got older we were allowed glimpses into Oz, Narnia, and Middle Earth. We traveled down a yellow brick road, met talking animals, and learned that the road goes ever on.

Books open paths to places that can't be reached in our day to day lives.

A literary theme baby shower calls for each guest to bring (in addition to their gift) a *special book* from their childhood; something that inspired them and, indeed, continues to hold a fond place in their heart after all of these years.

Although it will be years before the baby will be able to read any of these books; he or she will already have a treasured small library just waiting for them in the future. One of things that you can do during the shower is have everybody in the room tell why the book they brought is so special to them. Chances are, there will be a lot of nodding, and smiling, and maybe even a few tears, too (the good kind, of course!).

Listed below is an adorable poem you can use for your invitations for this theme:

Bring a Book

As (Mother-to-be's name) due date is coming near,
We're inviting friends and family dear.
To choose a favorite story or fairy tale
That you would like Baby _____ to hear.
Instead of a card, please let (mother-to-be's name)look,
At your special choice of a book,
and then to Baby _____ she will read
With all the love a newborn will need.
So with a personal touch, please choose a book

And in it then your name do put.
It need not cost more than a card
Just pick a favorite, it shouldn't be hard.
Author unknown

As you can see, a baby shower theme is only limited by your imagination and creativity. It doesn't have to be anything overly elaborate to be fun.

If you don't want to do a theme that is fine too. General decorations for the shower would generally be streamers and balloons. You can easily find both at any party store or general discount store. You can also easily find cups, plates, and napkins that are baby themed. Decorations do not have to be elaborate to make your room look very festive and the perfect atmosphere for your shower.

Setting Up Your Room

Give yourself plenty of time to set up and decorate for your shower. If possible set up the day before, but if not possible at least give yourself several hours. Examine your room and figure out the four primary questions that must be answered for set up:

- Where should I set up the gift table?
- Where will the food be set up?
- Where is everybody going to sit for games/socializing/watching gifts being opened/eating

You don't have to stress yourself out over set up for a baby shower, but it is a good idea to get a logistic picture in your head of where everything is going to happen. Many factors are of course going to determine how you set everything up. If you are holding the baby shower in your home, for example, you may be planning on having the food set up in the kitchen or dining room and the socializing to occur in the living room or den. If you are in a banquet hall or fellowship hall then you will most likely be in an open room and you will need to set up tables for the different things that will be going on.

49

You need to have an area for a gift table to be set up. This will be where everybody will place their presents when they come in. When the actual gift opening occurs you will want to make sure that mom has a seat near where all the gifts are and that it is a good location for everybody to be able to see as she opens the gifts. If you are having a large shower you may need two tables to be able to hold everything.

You also need to consider where the food is going to be set up. Since most food served at baby showers is finger foods (details on this later in the book) it is very easy to set up everything buffet style and have everybody serve themselves. Set up a table or two to hold everything. Place the plates, napkins, and utensils at the starting end of the table to direct the flow of the line the way it would be best for the location you are at. You might want to cut and serve the cake yourself (or recruit a volunteer). We will specifically discuss serving the cake in the Food section of the book. If you are going to be serving any food that needs to be kept warm, make sure you have easy access to an electrical outlet where your food is being served and make sure you have an extension cord if necessary.

Decide which part of the room will be best for the main seating area. Make sure that everybody will have a good view of the area where mom is going to sit and open gifts.

Having tables set up during your shower is going to be something you will have to determine based on your location and if you will have access to any. If you are holding the shower in a large room then having tables set up would be very nice. If you are in a smaller space then you may have to just set up chairs. If people aren't going to have a table to be able to set their plates and cups down on then make sure that the food you serve is indeed very simple and would involve no need of having to cut anything with a knife. Put plenty of space between the chairs so that everybody is not crammed together. Consider things such as purses and making sure they have enough room to sit them down beside them. When eating realize they may have to sit their drinks on the floor beside the chair and be sure and give them room to do so. If you don't have easy access to tables and chairs it is possible to rent them, but you will have to factor that decision into your budget cost.

In most cases you will probably not have a separate eating area for your shower. If by some chance you do then make sure that you direct everybody where they need to go and get food and where they need to go and eat.

If holding the shower in your home, make sure that you have enough places for everybody to be able to sit down. If your furniture won't be enough room then you will need to get access to some folding chairs. You always want to make sure that your guests have a chair to sit in. It is not proper for them to have to stand or to have to sit on the floor.

Logistics shouldn't be too difficult to figure out. Simply make sure that you utilize the space you have in the best way to keep everybody comfortable and to make sure that you don't have a lot of congested areas when people are up getting food and returning to their seats.

Games

Baby showers are great places to play games. Generally done at the very beginning of the shower, games are great way to break the ice and get everybody talking and laughing. Trying to think of games does not have to be stressful at all. They don't have to be elaborate and you don't have to do many of them. In fact it would be suggested to only do two or three games at the most. The main purpose of the shower is for everybody to be able to relax and socialize together. Doing too many games can make the shower feel too structured.

Always make sure that your games are in good taste and are not awkward or could potentially offend anyone. If planning any games that involve physical movement keep in mind the physical limitations of the mother-to-be and other guests in attendance. Have a couple of back up games ready, just in case you can sense that a game you have planned may not be going over well.

Listed below are some suggestions for games you can play during your shower.

Baby Crosswords or Word Search

If you have access to the web, this is one of the easiest games that you can do for your shower. There are many websites available that have baby themed crosswords and word searches that you can print out or make copies. (www.baby-shower-games-and-ideas.com is one such site)

Don't Say "Baby" Game

This game is fun and will really get people focused on talking and listening to each other! Not too long after the shower begins give everybody a certain amount of clothes pins (or safety pins) that they will clip to their clothes or hold. The number is up to you, but 4 or 5 is usually a good number. Tell everybody that they can't say the word "baby". For as long as the game is going on, if somebody catches another person saying the word "baby" then she gets to take that persons clothes pin and add it to her collection. At the end of the game the person with the most clothes pins wins and gets a prize. This game is perfectly fine to go on playing while the food is served and eaten. In fact when people are relaxed and talking is often when they slip up and say the forbidden word the most!

Guess the Baby Food Flavor

This game is quite hilarious to play. Get about 6 to 10 jars of baby food. (If you want to be merciful to the guests you can choose only fruits and veggies. If a little devil exists inside of you, include some of the mixed variety dinners ;-) Remove or completely cover the label of the baby food and number each jar starting with 1 and going through however many jars you have. Give each guest a pencil, paper, and small plate. Bring each numbered jar of food around and have everybody dip a little sample out on their plate. After tasting each sample they are to write the down on their paper the number of the jar and what they think the flavor is. The one who guesses the most flavors correctly is the winner and gets a prize! This game gives everybody a good understanding of some of the faces babies make when they eat!!

Guess Mommy's Tummy Size

If your mommy-to-be is a good sport about her growing tummy then this is a very fun game to play. Bring around to every person either a roll of toilet paper or yarn. Have them tear off or cut the amount of paper or yarn that they think it will take to wrap around to the center of mommy's tummy. After everybody has torn or cut off their amount let them test it on mom. The person who is the most accurate gets a prize.

Guess the Amount of Safety Pins

This game can be done as the guests are arriving. Have a container full of safety pins sitting on a table. Have a piece of paper and pen lying beside the jar. Have each person write her name down and their guess on how many pins are in the container. The person who makes the closest guess wins a prize.

Family Word Scramble

This game can be played if mom and dad have already picked a name out for the baby. Write the full name of the baby and also mom and dad on a piece of paper. Using the letters of their names have everybody write down as many new words as they can make out. This game is the most fun if it is timed. Give about a minute to come up with all the words they can. If you want to make it really challenging only give about 30 seconds. The person who writes down the most words wins a prize.

Diaper the Baby

This is a fun game to play in pairs. Have a table with a baby doll on it wearing a diaper. Place a new diaper on the table beside the doll. Have two people come up and make them each put an arm behind their back. Together their goal is to get the old diaper off the baby doll and then put the new one on. Time each pair and the pair that diapers the baby in the quickest amount of time wins the game and gets prizes. This game gets quite hilarious sometimes. Usually the first pair or two will try and treat the baby doll very gently. However the competitive people will get quite fierce and the way the poor baby doll gets tossed about gets quite funny to watch!

Prizes

There are two ways you can handle the prizes and either one is fine. The first way is to actually have true prizes for the people that win the games. They can be small, simple little items such as candy or small bottles of lotion. The second thing you can do is make all the prizes small but useful baby items such as diaper cream, pacifiers, washcloths, etc. Each person that wins the prize will then give their prize to mommy to be used for the baby.

Food

Food is one of the central things at a baby shower. Usually after the games are played then everybody gets the chance to eat and have a chance to sit around and talk to each other. Food is a very important part of the shower, but remember it does not have to be elaborate. Full course meals are generally not served at showers but instead most shower food is simple finger foods that can be easily prepared or bought. One key tip in planning food for the shower is check with the mother-to-be and make sure that she doesn't have any type of dietary restrictions. Gestational diabetes and other health factors can occur during pregnancy and require that mom have to carefully watch what she eats. Also pregnancy can cause women to have sensitive stomachs and certain foods may not agree with them. Now this does not mean that if mom is on a special diet that your entire guest list has to be put on one as well, but you do want to make sure that you do have some foods at the shower that mom can eat.

Listed on the next pages you will find a list of suggestions and recipes that can be served at your shower:

Croissant Sandwiches

Get a package of croissant rolls and make sandwiches with them. The easiest types of sandwiches to make with these are chicken, tuna, ham, or egg salad. Maybe get a couple of different salads to have a variety. Pimento cheese sandwiches are also easy to make and are another good variety to add to the salad sandwiches.

Little Smokies in Barbeque Sauce

This is a very simple recipe to make. Get packages of cocktail sausages. (The amount will depend on how many people are coming to the shower) Place in a crock pot and pour barbeque sauce over them. Heat until warm and viola you are done! Make sure you will access to an electrical outlet to be able to keep the smokies warm until right before you need to serve.

Pigs in a Blanket

Cocktail Sausages - (Look at package size to see how many are included per bag and base how many bags you buy on the number of guests coming to the shower)

Canned Crescent Rolls - (1 can generally makes 24 pigs in a blanket. Determine how many smokies you will have to determine how many cans of crescent rolls you will need)

Preheat oven to 350. Open crescent rolls and carefully unroll and separate each dough triangle. With a knife or pizza cutter cut each triangle vertically into three pieces. Place a cocktail sausage onto a dough piece and roll upwards. Place the sausages onto a baking sheet and bake for 8 to 10 minutes or until golden brown.

Sausage Balls

3 cups of baking mix (such as Bisquick)
1 lb. ground sausage
1 8 oz. package of cheddar cheese

Brown the sausage in a skillet. Drain the grease off and place in a large mixing bowl. Add the baking mix and cheese and mix well together with a large spoon or by hand. Form into small balls and place on an ungreased cookie sheet. Bake at 375 for about 15 minutes or until lightly browned.

Vegetable Tray

This one is very simple to have at a baby shower due to the fact that most grocery stores carry pre-made veggie trays and most often include dip. If you want to prepare yourself buy an assortment of vegetables and cut into slices. Popular vegetables for a tray include celery, carrots, raw broccoli, raw cauliflower, and cherry or grape tomatoes. Ranch dressing is a very popular dip for vegetables. You can either buy in bottles or make your own with the Hidden Valley Ranch packets.

Fruit Tray

Fruit trays are another item that most grocery stores carry pre-made. Popular fruits for a fruit tray are strawberries, apples, grapes, cantaloupe, and honey dew. A very simple but delicious dip is listed below:

Fruit Dip

8 oz. package cream cheese
1 small jar of marshmallow cream

Beat the cream cheese with a mixer until soft and smooth. Add the jar of marshmallow cream and mix well.

Chips and Dip

This is another classic shower food that requires no thought or preparation. You can find many containers of dip already made at the grocery store. If you want to make your own, listed below is a very simple and quick dip to make:

Onion Soup Dip

1 package onion soup mix
1 small container of sour cream

Mix onion soup mix and sour cream together and chill for about 20 minutes before serving.

The last finishing touches of food that you might want to have at a shower would be to buy a few cans of mixed nut and have them available for everyone and also if you can find them buy a can or two of the pastel butter mints.

Drinks

Punch is traditionally served at baby showers. It is not difficult to make punch and can be as easy as pouring carbonated fruit punch in a serving bowl and adding a container of sherbet to it. Listed below are a couple of punch recipes:

Punch Recipe 1

2 pkgs of cherry or strawberry Jell-O
1 cup hot water
2 quarts cold water
2 cups sugar
1 large can of pineapple juice
1 quart ginger ale
Sherbet- Any flavor desired

Pour the hot water into the punch bowl; add the 2 packages of Jell-O and dissolve completely. Add the sugar next while the mixture is still warm to help dissolve it as well. Add the cold water and pineapple juice and stir. Right before serving add the sherbet and then add the ginger ale.

Punch Recipe 2

1 tub of vanilla ice cream
1 2 liter of strawberry soda
2 8 oz. pkgs of frozen strawberries.

A day or two before serving, place strawberries in refrigerator to thaw. Set the ice cream out a little bit before serving and allow to soften so it is easy to get out of the container. In the punch bowl, place the thawed strawberries, and most of the softened ice cream. Pour the strawberry soda in the bowl and place remaining ice cream on top.

In addition to punch you might want to also have available various regular and diet sodas and water available for people that might not like punch or have a medical condition that would prevent them from drinking it.

The Cake

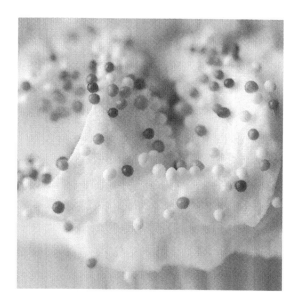

One food that is crucial to have at a shower is a cake. This should be very easy for you to obtain. Most local grocery stores have a bakery that you can order from or you can always go to a bakery specialty shop. Depending on the size of your guest list you can order a ¼, ½, or full sheet cake. Every place that you go should have a listing of the various ways that the cake can be decorated. Make sure that you order your cakes several weeks in advance of the shower. Some specialty bakeries require you to put in a cake order four to six weeks in advance. Most local grocery stores probably don't require that, but as a courtesy you might want to anyway. To do something different than a traditional cake you might also consider serving cupcakes at the shower. This can be a time saver if you have a lot of people and don't want to have to cut a lot of pieces of cake.

The cake can be served as everybody is coming through the food line and getting the rest of the food or you can have people come up and get cake after they finish eating. Choose whichever method will work best with the amount of people you have and the space you have. In smaller showers you can be more relaxed with things. Larger showers or tighter spaces however require a more streamlining process of everything. If your shower is small it shouldn't be a problem to cut and serve pieces of cake to people as they come through the line. If you have a lot of people attending however, it might be a smart idea to recruit a volunteer to go ahead and starting cutting the cake and putting it on plates while the games are going on. This will allow people to simply grab a plate of cake as they are going through the food line and keep the line from getting too congested.

If there is a designated photographer at the shower be sure and let her take pictures of the cake before you cut into it. Always make sure that mom and dad are served the first pieces of cake.

Food preparation does not have to be elaborate at the shower. Cake, chips and dip, and punch are perfectly acceptable to serve if you don't have the time or the budget to do anything else. If you want to be more creative then absolutely feel free to do so. Just make sure that you have enough for everybody. Your guest list will be a great guide for how much food to have and then just to be safe go over a little more. As stated you can always have that unexpected person or two who makes a last minute decision to come to the shower. It is always better to err on the side of having too much food then not enough.

Opening Gifts

Watching mom open up all the presents is of course the central activity of the baby shower. After everybody is finished eating is generally when this part of the shower occurs. In your setup you picked the ideal location where the gift table should go. So, at this stage in the shower you lead mom over to where she will sit and open gifts. Everything is downhill for you from here on out. You don't have to do much for this part of the shower, but there are a couple of key things that you will want to make sure are done.

- Have somebody available to hand the presents to mom so that she can open them.
- Make sure to have somebody designated to write down who each gift is from and what the gift is. The parents are going to want to send out thank

you cards and it is important to help them keep track of everything. If you mailed out invitations you should already have a list of all the guest's addresses. If by chance you invited everybody by phone then make sure you get everybody's full address before they leave the shower so that the parents will have a record.

Clean-Up

Once the gifts are open and everybody has had a chance to ooh and aahh over everything, the shower should naturally start to wind down.

Even if you have helpers with the clean-up, don't start the clean-up process until everybody is gone. You are the hostess until the last person has left and even at the end you don't want to give the impression that you are trying to rush anybody out the door. Make yourself available to help mom and dad carry all the gifts out to their vehicle. Once they are gone then you can go back inside and begin the clean-up process.

If you are holding the shower in a banquet hall, fellowship hall, restaurant or any other outside location be sure and follow all rules and guidelines that were given to you regarding clean-up. Make sure you give yourself plenty of time for clean-up when setting the time for your reservation.

Before you do any cleaning though be sure and reach around and give yourself a HUGE pat on the back. You did it!! You organized and pulled off an incredible baby shower. Clean up, go home, and relax knowing a job has been well done. Don't get too comfortable though. Now

71

that everybody knows what a great shower you can throw, you may just have people contacting you to do more!!

Part 3: Frequently Asked Questions

Hopefully the previous pages have been useful and helpful to you in planning your shower. Just in case something might not have been covered in the previous sections, listed below are some frequently asked questions and other general tips that might be of further help to you in planning your shower

Question: *Should the shower just be for mom or should dad be invited as well?*

A few years ago when you heard the words "baby shower" you could pretty much guarantee the fact that dad would not be there. Society has changed a lot over the past few years. Dad used to not be allowed into the delivery room either but now it is pretty much standard practice that he will be there at the birth of his child. Baby showers have changed over the years as well and it is no longer a given that dad won't be at the shower.

It is absolutely wonderful and perfectly acceptable to have a shower for both mom and dad. Some men are still traditionalists and want nothing to do with a baby shower, but if you can get dad there then absolutely do so!

So if dad is coming does this change anything as far as your planning goes? Yes, it does. Not in a huge way, but there are definitely some factors that you want to consider if dad is going to be at the shower.

The Guest List – If dad is coming to the shower then you might want to consider inviting some of his male friends to come as well so that he won't be the only male in a room full of women. However don't automatically assume that he will want this and be sure to check with him and mom before you start inviting people. If you are planning on inviting other males to the shower be sure and somehow let your invitations reflect this. Men coming to baby showers are an idea that is gaining popularity in our society but it has not gotten to the point yet where that is the standard. Most women who receive a baby shower invitation would not automatically assume that men will be coming as well. It could cause awkwardness if people don't know ahead of time that the shower will be co-ed so to speak.

The Season – We've talked about Christmas and we've talked about winter, but if men are going to come to a shower then there is something else we have to talk about and that is sports. Many men don't just like sports, they love sports. Many men will indeed plan their lives around certain sporting events and if you make the grave error of trying to plan a baby shower on one of those key sporting event days, you could have a black checkmark by your name **FOREVER**. For example, Super Bowl Sunday would probably not be the best day to have a baby shower if you wanted to have any chance of having males show up. When you are planning on the date for your shower be sure and check with dad and find out if there are any sport related conflicts that might occur with him. He will be extremely grateful for your consideration and he will also probably be truly touched at how much you are including him in the process.

Themes – If men are going to be at the shower you might want to make sure that your theme is not too frilly and more gender neutral. Dad and his friends simply might not appreciate the concept of dressing up in pink clothes like mom and her friends would for a baby girl theme.

Question: *Are surprise baby showers acceptable or should mom always be informed?*

As a general rule it is not a good idea to throw a surprise baby shower. The entire focus of the shower should be about the parents-to-be and as we've discussed through-out the entire book getting their input on the decisions you make is invaluable. Also, something that you com-pletely risk in planning a surprise shower is that you could get everything planned and find out that you have chosen a time that is completely inconvenient for them and they might not be able to come.

Question: *How long should the baby shower last?*

As a general rule of thumb two or three hours is a good time frame for a baby shower. If a shower gets too long then people can start getting bored or restless. You should definitely include a clear beginning and ending time on the invitations that you send out. People need to be able to plan their day out and so they need to have a time frame of when the shower is going to end. Going over time by a few minutes is certainly not anything to get frantic over, and you as the hostess don't want to ever give the impression that you are trying to rush the shower along, but you do want to keep a monitor on the time as the shower is going along. If you are renting the space where the shower is being held you will have to keep a tighter rein on time. Many places reserve multiple gatherings a day and yours might not be the only one scheduled.

One thing that you might want to do right at the beginning is look at how many presents mom has to open. The opening of gifts is generally what takes the longest amount of time at the shower. Mom of course wants to admire everything that is opened and generally the other guests do as well. If you can see that mom has a huge amount of presents to open and you are worried that it might run the shower too far over time then you might want to consider cutting out a game if you have multiple ones planned.

Question: *Should a baby shower only be thrown for the first baby?*

In the past, it was considered proper to only throw a baby shower for the first baby. Once again, society has changed over the years and now it is considered perfectly acceptable and appropriate to throw a shower for every child that is born to a couple. They will have just as much joy over the second and third child as they did over the first child. So if you want to host a shower for a second, third, or even fourth child then by all means do so!

Question: *Is an adoption shower a good idea?*

Absolutely!! Parents that are expecting a child by adoption are filled with the same joy as parents that are having a child naturally. Adoptive parents need all the same items for the baby.

In the case of an adoption shower though it is honestly a better idea to have the shower after the baby is born and the parents actually have their child. It doesn't happen often, but adoptions sometimes do fall through. It would be devastating to parents to have gone through the joy and excitement of a shower and then the adoption not happen.

Couples in the United States often adopt children from other countries. The red tape that is involved in this process can take years for an adoption to actually occur. Once their baby is finally born it may be months before the parents can finally bring the baby home. Waiting in this case would be a necessity so everyone would be able to buy age appropriate items.

Question: *Should children be allowed to come to the baby shower?*

The answer to this question is a bit of a delicate one and should absolutely be left up to the mommy-to-be. Traditionally, children do not usually come to baby showers. They can of course be very energetic and if there is not enough activity going on that they find interesting then they could become bored with the whole process. It could become distracting to everyone if an unhappy child is in attendance.

However, some guests might not be able to attend if they can't bring their children, so this is something that you absolutely must discuss with the mom-to-be and see how she wants to handle the situation. If children are coming you definitely want to think about this as you come up with activities. You might want to have some coloring pages or other activities they can do while the other activities of the shower are going on.

Part 4:
Checklists/Planners

This final section of the book contains various checklists and planners that you can use to help plan and organize your baby shower

Use them in any way that you need to and make as many copies as you need. These are yours to use however you see fit.

If you are reading this book as a digital download you can access these planners by visiting the following link:

http://babyshowerplanning.org/planner/planners.pdf

The documents are in a PDF file that you can either print or save to your computer

Shower Agenda

Event	Time	Details
Welcome		
Icebreaker		
Guest of Honor		
Game(s)		
Food		
Gifts		
Wrap Up		

Guest List

Name	Telephone #	Email Address	RSVP

Supply List

Item Needed	Location	Price
Guest Book/Sign In Sheet		
Decorations		
Food		
Dessert		
Plates		
Utensils		
Serving Utensils		
Drinks		
Cups		
Ice		
Napkins		
Games / Supplies		
Camera		
Video Camera		
Scissors		
Tape		
Cleaning Supplies		
Trash Bag(s)		

Shower Budget

Description of Expenses Drinks/Food: Appetizers, Meal, Cake, Caterer	Projected Costs	Actual Costs

Description of Expenses Party Goods: Invitations, Plates, Napkins, Decorations	Projected Costs	Actual Costs

Description of Expenses Entertainment: Games, Prizes	Projected Costs	Actual Costs

Description of Expenses Rental: Hall, Restaurant,	Projected Costs	Actual Costs

Shower Planner A

Name of Mommy-To-Be:	Name of Host(s) :	Date of Shower:
		RSVP By Date:
Location:	Contact Phone #:	Contact Email Address:
Directions to Shower:	Registry Location(s):	Baby Room Theme:
Dress: Formal / casual	Shower Theme:	Baby Details (due date/sex):

Guests to Invite

1.	11.
2.	12.
3.	13.
4.	14.
5.	15.
6.	16.
7.	17.
8.	18.
9.	19.
10.	20.

Foods / Drinks to Serve

1.	6.
2.	7.
3.	8.
4.	9.
5.	10.

Shower Checklist

ONE MONTH BEFORE	THREE WEEKS BEFORE	TWO WEEKS BEFORE
___ Create a Budget ___ Choose Theme ___ Make the Guest List ___ Make or Buy Invitations ___ Create Menu ___ Make Shopping List ___ Choose Games	___ Send Invitations ___ Rent any Equipment ___ Buy Decorations ___ Order Food ___ Order Supplies	___ Order Cake ___ Order Flowers ___ Organize and prepare supplies for games
ONE WEEK BEFORE	TWO DAYS BEFORE	ONE DAY BEFORE
___ Buy Food & Drink ___ Buy Thank You Cards ___ Call Non RSVP guests ___ Make Shower Timeline	___ Buy Garbage Bags ___ Arrange for someone to write gift list ___ Choose Party Music	___ Clean Party Area ___ Charge Video Camera ___ Decorate for Shower ___ Set up Games / Activities ___ Prepare Food that can refrigerate well
PARTY DAY!	DAY AFTER PARTY	NOTES
___ Pick up Cake, Ice ___ Prepare Food ___ Finish Decorating ___ Prepare Cake Table ___ Set up Presents Area & Get Gifts Rec'd List Ready ___ Get Camera Ready	___ Return Rented / Borrowed Equipment ___ Throw Away Whatever you Don't intend to use again ___ Download / Develop Photos	

Shower Planner B

Guests to Invite

1.	11.
2.	12.
3.	13.
4.	14.
5.	15.
6.	16.
7.	17.

Foods / Drinks to be Served

1.	6.
2.	7.
3.	8.
4.	9.

Party Prep	Completed	Instructions / Notes
Choose Date & Location		
Decide if Formal / Informal, Potluck / Buffet / Sit-down		
Make/Buy & Send Invitations		
Choose Games &/or Music		
Clean House & Decorate House OR		
Prepare Menu		
Make Shopping List		
Go Shopping		
Prepare Food		

Shower Planner C

Mother-To-Be:	Shower Date/Time:
Father-To-Be:	Due Date:
Gender:	Baby's Name:
Colors/Theme:	Location:

Guests:

Menu:

Dishes	Drinks	Sweets

Ingredients	Supplies

Schedule of Events:
1.
2.
3.
4.
5.
Comments:

Day of Shower Timeline

Time	Day of Shower Plan	Notes
:00		
:30		
:00		
:30		
:00		
:30		
:00		
:30		
:00		
:30		
:00		
:30		
:00		
:30		
:00		
:30		
:00		
:30		
:00		
:30		
:00		

Shower Preparation

1. Prepare a Budget and stick to it!

---

2. Decide on Theme or Style (Formal/Informal, Sit-Down/Buffet/Potluck).

---

3. Decide on Date for Shower. Choose a Start and End time so guests are clear.

---

4. Decide on Location (Home, Restaurant, Business, Outdoors).

---

5. Make the Guest List.

---

6. Create a Menu.

---

7. Make Grocery Shopping List OR Arrange for Catering.

---

8. Buy or Make Invitations.

---

9. Send Invitations 3 weeks before Shower.

---

10. Make a Cleaning List OR Arrange for Cleaning Service.

---

11. Consider Parking. Make Arrangements.

---

12. Be Prepared for Accidents and Spills. Have Spot Cleaner, Dish Towels, & Blankets ready.

---

13. Before Guests arrive, Relax & Breathe!!

Gifts Received

Gift	From	Store for Return (just in case)	Thank You Sent

Food & Fun Worksheet

Food / Drinks	Ingredients Needed	Instructions

Games / Activities	Supplies Needed	Instructions

Made in the USA
Lexington, KY
01 February 2013